Grace Learns About

Chaharshanbe Souri

Grace Learns About
Chaharshanbe-Souri

Written by Ellie Fard

Illustrations by Somayeh Royaee
Copyright © Ellie Fard 2021

ISBN : 9798585440205

Chaharshanbe-Souri, or the festival of fire, is an ancient Persian festival held on the last Wednesday of the Iranian calendar year.

It symbolizes good health, light, and purity.

In the afternoon, people gather brushwood and by night they light bonfires in open areas. They jump over the flames and sing a special song. This song means, I wish the fire would take all our sickness, and problems and turn them to warmth, energy, and health.

It also symbolizes the readiness for a new spring and a new start.

Persian trick or treating is called Ghashogh Zani, which means "spoon banging." it resembles a blend of Halloween and New Year's Eve.

Children wear masks and go door to door, banging spoons against bowls to receive nuts, snacks, and sweets.

I hope children enjoy learning this celebration with Grace!

Grace Learns About Chaharshanbe-Souri

Today is the first day of school year.

Grace and Mom are walking to school.

Pre-school

Miss Ellie is welcoming everyone at the front door.

It is a good day to meet old friends and make new ones.

Everyone lines up outside the classroom.

They go inside and...

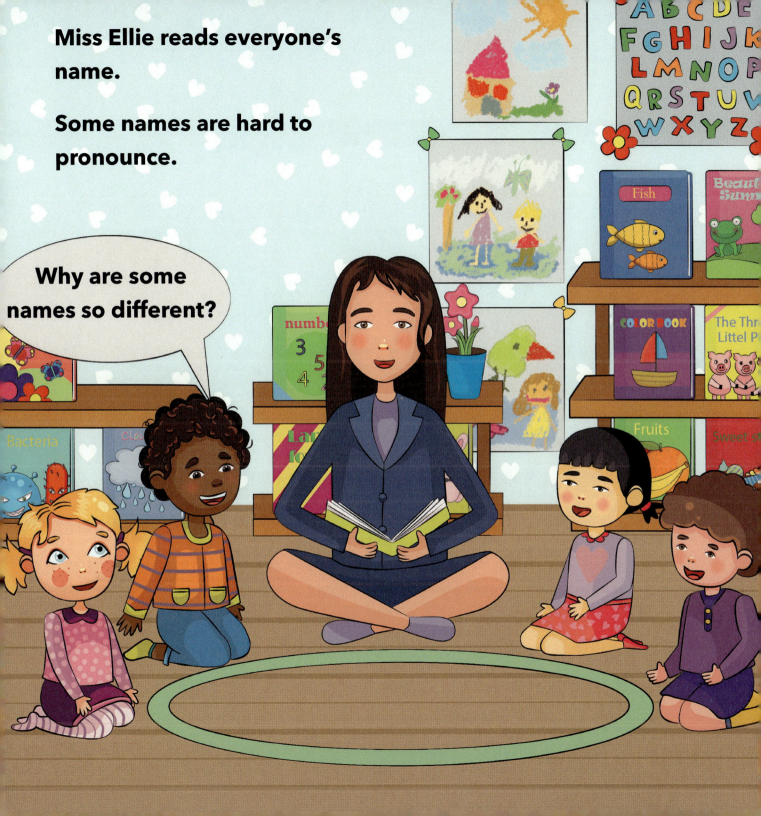

We have a diverse class

Miss Ellie smiles.

"What does diverse mean?" Grace asks.

Miss Ellie says,"It means that People are different. Everyone is special and no one is better than the others."

"How are they different?" Chen asks.

"Everyone, show me your fist," says Miss Ellie.

Everyone makes a fist. They see their hands look different.

" We have different skin colors, we eat different foods, we have different names, and we celebrate different things!"

It is called diversity.

Grace raised her hand.

" I know a Persian celebration! It is called Chaharshanbe-Souri "

"Can you tell us more about it?"

Miss Ellie asked.

"Well, I don't know much."Grace said.

"Maybe we can learn more about it soon." Miss Ellie said.

At circle time next morning,
Mom was sitting next to Grace.

She had a basket full of nuts,
spoons, masks and candles.

What are those?

Then Mom started to tell the story of Chaharshanbe-Souri.

The last Wednesday of the Persian calendar is a special day.

It is the festival of fire.

Last Wednesday Of Year

Neighbors knock on each other's door and invite the whole neighborhood to a celebration in the street.

There is fire, dancing and singing.

Everyone, old and young, jumps over the fire and sings:

" Sorkhi-e to az man   Zardi-e man az to "

(Which means :Your redness is mine and my paleness is yours.!)

Children wear masks and go trick or treating!

They all have small bowls and a spoon to bang on it!

treats are a handful of nuts or sweets.

"That looks like fun to me." Miss Ellie said.

"I know today is not the last Wednesday of year, but can we pretend it is?"

Everyone shouted "YES!".

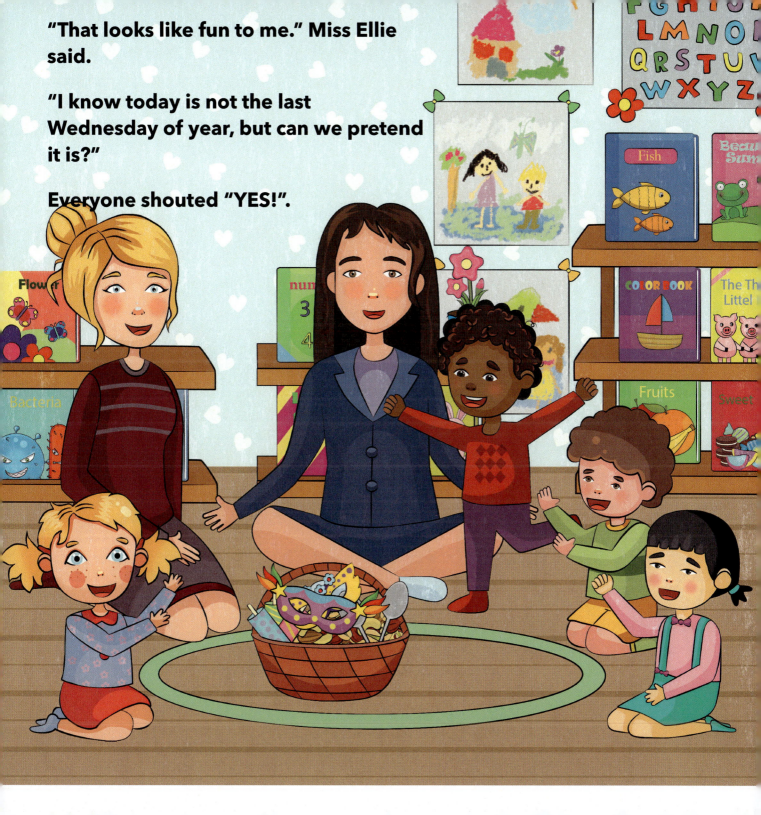

Everyone was excited to pick a mask, spoon, and bowl to go trick or treating!

Mom pretends to be a neighbor . It is funny.

We set pretend candles in the school yard to jump over.

It is even more fun when you hold hands with a friend and sing the song!

You can wish everyone a healthy year ahead.

(Sorkhi-e to az man   Zardi-e man az to)

Happy
Chaharshanbe-Souri

List of Persian Festivals:

-Nourooz: It means starting a new day and it is the celebration of the start of spring. It starts on the first day of spring (also the first day of the Iranian calendar year), March 21. All Iranian families gather around and visit each other for 12 days.

-Sizdah Bedar: Known as nature day, is an Iranian festival held annually on thirteenth day of spring. It marks the end of Nourooz holidays in Iran and people spend time picnicking outdoors.

-Yalda Night: The longest night of the year.

- Chaharshanbe-Souri: Festival of fire, the last Wednesday night in the Iranian calendar year. It marks the importance of the light over the darkness, arrival of spring and revival of nature.

You May Also Like These:

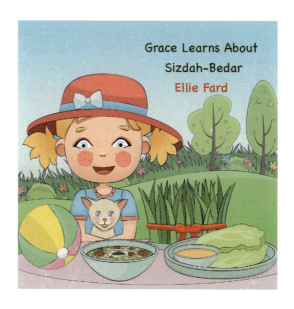

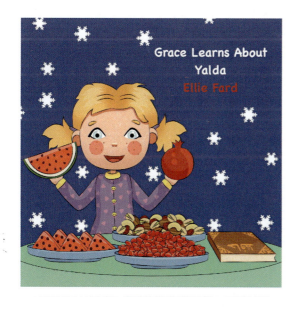

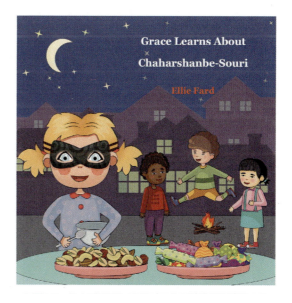

Made in the USA
Las Vegas, NV
17 March 2025

19719012R00017